FROM THE INSIDE OUT

Katherine Kim

DESTRUCTION ANGER EATING DISORDERS ARROGANCE TEMPTATION

ISBN: 979-8-35094-509-6

FROM THE INSIDE OUT

Katherine Kim

"You gain strength, courage and confidence by every experience in which you really stop to look fear in the face. You are able to say to yourself, 'I have lived through this horror. I can take the next thing that comes along.' You must do the thing you think you cannot do."

— ELEANOR ROOSEVELT

CONTENTS

INTRODUCTION

The COVID-19 virus officially crossed into the United States in January 2020 and became a full-blown pandemic in April 2020. The virus not only affected our health and our approach to it; it also transformed every aspect of our lives, including economics, politics, education, business, and all activities of daily living. The COVID-19 pandemic was also a global phenomenon that simultaneously united and divided the world. As difficult as the years 2020 and 2021 were for many, we had to quickly adapt to an unfamiliar circumstance and not be affected by this disease physically, emotionally, or spiritually.

After health officials declared that the COVID-19 outbreak was a pandemic, I was forced to deal with many changes in my personal life. My school switched to online learning, I could no longer see my friends as easily, and I did not have my middle school graduation ceremony. Instead, I have photos of my class on a computer screen. I was also unable to visit my grandparents in South Korea for a couple of years because there were so many restrictions on traveling and immigration policies that varied wildly from country to country. I began my freshman year of high school with a drive-thru orientation and therefore did not have the chance to meet new friends in person. Seniors lined up in the school parking lot with greeting signs and club posters, cheering for us as we drove by. At the end of the line, I opened the window and they handed me a welcome package. That was the beginning of my high school years.

As the pandemic continued to force people to stay together at home, many of our daily activities had to be taken care of online. People were working from home, students were taking classes online, and churches were conducting services and small group meetings through the Internet. We all became accustomed to online shopping and public services. Because the law required us to maintain social distance when we did leave our homes, an invisible emotional distance wedged itself into any sort of interaction. While we responded to the pandemic differently and in our own unique ways, it was a tough transition for all of us. One valuable lesson that the COVID-19 pandemic taught me was that I can succeed in life if I adjust my attitude and respond accordingly to any situation. I could do nothing to alter the spread of the virus worldwide or influence the rules and regulations that arose from the pandemic, but I tried to change how I responded to my circumstances. I tried to make the best of it. For example, I tried hard to make online learning work for me by actively engaging with my teachers and classmates in the virtual classroom and participating in as many school activities as I could do online. I also tried to make our family time more memorable. Our family, as well as many other families, could not enjoy a meal at a restaurant anymore. So we celebrated our birthdays at home baking and cooking. We now share so many good memories of celebrating our birthdays, Thanksgiving, and Christmas together at home.

I have compiled a series of stories and anecdotes of these teaching moments of my life and I am honored to celebrate my memories with you. Despite the restrictions on our past way of living, I continued to navigate new paths toward improving my life and serving the community. I maintained my connections to various nonprofit organizations throughout the pandemic. Through these organizations, I was able to teach underserved students in Phoenix, Arizona, how to play musical instruments (drums, guitar, and clarinet), along with various academic subjects, especially mathematics. However, our relationships became more than just a tutor–student dynamic, and I was asked to share my stories with the students. I now look forward to sharing these stories and my journey with you.

OHANA

Most people believe that their families are unique and set apart. Any family holds fast to its own set of traditions, customs, values, and events that are integral to its history and interrelationships. These building blocks of a family include certain religious beliefs, yearly visits with grandparents, special holiday celebrations, and simple things like sharing a daily meal. All of these beloved aspects of family life came undone for many people when the coronavirus pandemic descended upon the world in 2020, the first one since the influenza pandemic in 1918. It was a globally challenging time for all aspects of society, but it was particularly difficult for many people at the family level—fathers and mothers lost their jobs, students in all grades were forced to participate in asynchronous learning, and incoming high school freshmen across the country had to experience one of their most pivotal years of life online.

In spite of all this, especially having to enter high school through the Internet, I am grateful to God that we were able to persevere through the COVD-19 pandemic. If not for the pandemic, my family might not have experienced the wonderful transformation that it did, my heart might not have been softened to accept the truth and change, and my physical health might have continued on its pre-pandemic downward spiral. Don't get me wrong—the isolation and the toll COVID-19 took on my mental health was not fun and I would not wish that experience on my worst enemy. However, when I look back on 2020 today after gaining perspective over the past few years, the long-term manifestations of the pandemic have been nothing but blessings for me as I look forward to the rest of my life. I will delve deeper into what exactly those blessings are and why I consider them as such. I would also like to share with you how those blessings have shaped me physically and spiritually and how they have established in me a firm foundation for the rest of my life.

One of those blessings is how COVID-19 affected my family. We were thrust into a situation that we had no control over, as were most people, and we used our creativity and resourcefulness to navigate our way through it. The pandemic not only brought us together by keeping us physically in the house, but we were able to hone our creativity and uncover valuable attributes about ourselves that will help us in the future. Through resilience, we were able to make the best of a rough circumstance.

As a thirteen-year-old, I was certain that my family was fairly close-knit, a family that rejoiced in one another's successes and commiserated together in our failures, a family that listened to each other, and a family that simply cared for one another. I wanted this sort of close relationship with my family and I truly believe that my family had a special bond that was beyond that of other families. However, when March 2020 came and went and the world was descending into the chaos that would become the COVID-19 pandemic, I came to the realization that I would have to spend every waking moment with my family, initially for two weeks as most experts at that time predicted. However, it was clear that the coronavirus was not going away anytime soon and we would continue to feel the reverberations of the pandemic in the years to come.

I understood that I would be isolated with my family in my house for an indefinite amount of time. I always thought that my brother was cute and adorable, but now his loud and obnoxious dialogue with his gaming friends would be a daily part of my life as well. As I was listening to my brother engage in an intense gaming session next door, I came to a startling yet inevitable revelation—the only form of meaningful social interaction I would have for the remainder of this so-called pandemic was the cashier at the grocery store and my immediate family members. What happened in the next few months confirmed not only that my family did have a special bond, but that through that bond we were able to forge a deeper and more satisfying relationship with one another as we were locked up together in the house. The first step was navigating an important series of dates immediately following the outbreak of the pandemic—our birthdays.

My mother's birthday is April 30. Mother's Day 2020 was on May 10, my brother's birthday is June 9, Father's Day was on June 21, my birthday is July 17, and my father's birthday is September 10. Governor Doug Ducey officially ordered all Arizonans to stay at home and effectively shut the state down on March 30, 2020, allowing only essential workers to continue working. Therefore, these important dates in our lives immediately followed the outbreak of the pandemic as Arizona was about to enter two months of an official lockdown. As confusing and chaotic as the world seemed at that time, we were able to block out the noise and focus on these dates as more than simply an excuse to buy gifts—we decided to make events out of them.

My parents, like most parents of teenagers who have probably had their share of birthday parties, never wanted to do anything spectacular to celebrate their birthdays. Whenever my brother and I would ask them what they wanted for their birthdays, they would always respond with a simple "nothing" and then say that they only asked that we continued to behave like godly men and women and showed kindness toward one another. On the other hand, my brother and I were young and wanted what most children wanted on their birthdays—a big birthday party with all of our friends. Because our birthdays were in the summer, my brother and I often celebrated while we were traveling on vacation. While we did not get to have our big birthday celebrations with our friends as often as we would have liked, we still enjoyed spending our birthdays on our trips away from home in foreign countries. But it was clear that the summer of 2020 was going to be unlike any other summer in history.

In that summer of 2020, we would not be traveling due to all of the travel restrictions, and we would be spending our summer not exploring a foreign culture, but in the comfort of our home. The huge birthday parties my brother and I desired probably would not happen either because public health officials advised us to stay away from each other, although the restrictions in Arizona were not as strict as those in other states. This was certainly demoralizing for us—no birthday parties and no traveling—yet it stirred our creative energy. These unfortunate circumstances gave our family no other choice but to celebrate our birthdays at home with only each other for company.

Food was often the language of love in our family. We expressed love to one another in many ways, through words of affirmation, quality time together, giving and receiving gifts, and serving the community together. But it was through the time spent on preparing and enjoying meals together that our family bonded. My mother would always and continues to make breakfast for my brother and me before we went to school, I would regularly bake a variety of pastries and cakes, and my father would grill his famous rib eye steaks with onions and asparagus every Saturday night for dinner. While I have fond memories of sharing these meals at home, my family also enjoyed dining out, from elegant restaurants to quick fast-food joints. We loved the sophisticated dining experience at a Michelin star restaurant, but we also cherished picking up a couple of Big Macs from McDonalds or ordering takeout from Papa John's. In a nutshell, our lives revolved around food.

The onset of the pandemic not only brought about drastic and lasting changes to the restaurant industry; it shook up the foundation of our family as well. One of the most memorable aspects of our travels was the variety of cuisines we were able to taste, from authentic Mexican to Chinese to Icelandic. Not only were we unable to travel, we also could not enjoy new and exotic food. In addition, as the restaurant industry came to a screeching halt, it was difficult to even get hamburgers for takeout. Many dine-in restaurants closed permanently and take-out meal transactions had to be done with a mask and through social distancing, a weird phenomenon in itself. Drive-thru services were temporarily halted and a whole host of regulations was instituted regarding food delivery. It did not help that we knew very little about the coronavirus itself. If we had known then what we know now, perhaps many of the draconian measures would not have been employed. Regardless of how things should have gone and how they actually did transpire, the restaurant and food industry was forever radically altered and we all had to adapt. As the world adapted, our family had no choice but to adjust and stir up our creative juices. All of the cooking we had done until then had been a practice run for the big game—gourmet meals at home during lockdown.

Mother's Day was the first "at-home" pandemic event that my father, my brother, and I attempted to make as grand as we had in previous years without going to a restaurant. As has always been the Kim family tradition, we blended my mother's birthday with Mother's Day due to the proximity of dates (April 30 and May 10). A week prior to Mother's Day, my dad and I texted back and forth nonstop, discussing how we were going to make this plan work. Although our family cooked for each other very often, we never had to cook a meal for a special occasion to be served in our very own home (we left that to the professional chefs at the restaurants we went to). We decided on a simple and easy menu that both my dad and I knew we could execute to perfection: filet mignons served with roasted potatoes and asparagus and a pasta with red meat sauce.

Online classes by nature are difficult to get through, but when you add the anticipation of preparing a three-course gourmet meal for your mother, it is extremely difficult to concentrate that entire week. In between quizzes about the Krebs Cycle and geometry proofs, I could not stop thinking about how I would plate the dish, what drinks I would serve with the food, and what kind of place mats would be the best fit for the occasion. Saturday was the day before Mother's Day, and it was also the day my father and I decided to shop for the groceries we needed to bring about our Mother's Day dinner. My brother stayed home with my mother while my father and I geared up in our N95 masks to head to the grocery store. As soon as we stepped foot inside the store, my dad and I diverged as I headed straight to the produce section and my dad headed to the meat section. After we finished grabbing all of the ingredients needed for the menu, we headed to the drinks aisle and picked out the most luxurious-looking orange juice and apple cider. We even picked out a bouquet of radiant pink roses to garnish the dinner table. When we arrived home, we took off our masks and hid the groceries in the refrigerator located in the garage.

I woke up the next morning barely able to contain my excitement about what would be going down later that night. My brother and I agreed to act as if we had forgotten our mother's birthday and Mother's Day and not mention anything until dinnertime. After our family watched our church's live-streamed service on YouTube, we waited patiently until it was time to begin cooking. Our original plan was to start preparing the food at 4:00 p.m. However, my father and I, being the overthinkers we are, decided to have an early dinner and start preparing the food at 2:00 p.m. I wanted the entire dinner to be a surprise and truly wanted to impress my mother with a home-cooked dinner she had never had, so I locked her in her room and told her that she could not come out of her room until I allowed her to do so. I was thirteen years old and wanted to completely knock my mom off her feet with the food that I would be making for her, so I was not going to compromise secrecy at any cost.

My dad grilled the filet mignons on a stovetop pan by basting them in rosemary and butter before tossing them into the oven. My brother's nick-name growing up was Carb Man because of the copious amounts of pasta, bread, pizza, and rice he would consume, so we put him in charge of the one thing he knew how to eat and cook the best—pasta. I set the table with place mats, silverware, roses, and drinks. I then tossed my mini potatoes into the air fryer with olive oil, garlic salt, Italian seasoning, and a hint of lemon zest. I describe creating this dinner menu as smooth and effortless, but at the moment, it was far from it. My dad and I were sweating from the heat of the kitchen and my brother (being the impatient ten-year-old he was) kept taking off the lid of the pot in which he was boiling pasta. The pasta did not get a chance to fully cook. In addition, the side dishes for the steak were getting cold because we had not timed the entire process thoroughly.

Despite our amateurish timing and preparation methods, we were able to get all of the food on the plates and make the table look spectacular. After preparations were completed and we were ready to eat, I instructed my mother, father, and brother to dress up in their nicest outfits and come out to the dinner table when they were ready. My mom was perplexed and could not help but wonder what her family was up to. She had smelled the juicy and tender steak from her bedroom for three hours and looked relieved to be allowed to come out of captivity. The look on my mother's face when she came out of her room made the entire process worth it, and it felt so rewarding knowing that she was impressed with our first attempt ever to create a memorable Mother's Day from home. We indulged in the delicious food—the filet mignons were so incredibly succulent it felt like I was biting into a stick of butter, my brother's pasta was just right, and my potatoes, onions, and asparagus were all seasoned correctly and cooked to perfection. The experience of preparing that COVID-19 Mother's Day dinner sparked my interest in cooking beyond baking cakes. The shutdown imposed on us did not seem so formidable now. I felt myself becoming a chef in my own right and I was looking forward to preparing more dining experiences for our family, no matter the length of the pandemic.

Mother's Day Dinner:

My Dad's Birthday Dinner:

After the monumental success of our Mother's Day/mother's birthday dinner, we honed our skills as chefs and prepared more meals on the other special dates we had lined up. It was a blessing to create those memorable experiences. We also engaged in another activity that seemed mundane before the pandemic but affected us in a profound way—hiking.

While hiking itself is not an extraordinary activity for any family to partake in, hiking during the coronavirus shutdown was a special experience for our family. Until the pandemic suddenly upended our lives, I had always believed that I was spending an adequate amount of time with my family and that I had a fairly good idea of who my family was. However, it was through these regular hikes with my family that I discovered the value of spending quality time with people that I thought I knew, but whom I can get to know in a deeper and more profound way.

Waking up early at 5:30 a.m. to escape the heat and getting dressed as my eyes were barely open was a double-edged experience; I hated and loved it at the same time. Waking up early was important in Arizona because the summer days of 110 degrees Fahrenheit were fast approaching, and it was necessary to do our hiking before our health and safety became an issue due to the heat. My brother and I were always in a grumpy mood toward the beginning of the hike because of how tired we were and how overwhelming it was to even think about hiking the entire trail. However, there was never a time when we finished a hike and came home feeling the same way we had in the morning. We became energized not only because of the strenuous trails and the cold Gatorade running through our systems during the hike, but also because of the meaningful conversations our family had as we huffed and puffed our way to the finish line. We would talk about how we would spend the rest of our day, how absurd it was that COVID-19 came into existence so abruptly, and how we needed to exercise more because these hikes exposed how out of shape we all were.

Our conversations were not always heavy and serious. We often reminisced about all of the silly and sensational moments of our lives up until that point. Reliving those moments was not only enjoyable, but it also allowed us to truly appreciate how fortunate we were as a family to have those memories. I also began grasping how relationships work and why relationships are so important for healthy living. My mother and father would frequently engage in conversations with me and my brother through the questions they asked us during these hikes. My parents always seemed so much wiser and smarter than us, which is why I believed that there was no point in answering these questions because they would already know what I or my brother was going to say. I realized they did not necessarily want answers to questions, but they wanted to hear our answers, and that creates relational bonds between friends and family. I learned so much about my parents and my brother that I never knew even though I had been living with them my entire life. I learned about their thoughts and feelings, their way of thinking, their way of approaching questions, their goals in life, and even their different mannerisms. It was not the answers to the questions that were so eye-opening, but the forging of relationships. What was happening in our family was a blessing born through the pandemic.

For the first time, I glimpsed the goals, plans, and intentions of my family members. I never thought of my mother or father as having dreams and aspirations; they were just Mom and Dad to me. I could never have imagined that my brother had goals he wanted to accomplish; he was just a younger brother who played video games. These awakening moments I had with my family not only compelled me to listen more to what they had to say, but also provoked me to realize that I never truly listened. We were a close family who cared deeply for one another; there is no doubt about this. However, even as a thirteen-year-old, I was excessively ambitious and not even remotely curious about what my mother, father, or brother were going through. I began to view my family not only in terms of what they were to me, but as whole human beings in their own right. I always believed that it was parents' duty to be strong for their children and put up a facade during their toughest times to hide their vulnerability. But my parents sharing with us not only their dreams and aspirations, but their vulnerabilities and fears, did not weaken them in my eyes but actually strengthened our relationship. Our regular hikes taught me how to be present for those you love and that being vulnerable is not a bad thing. This is not to say that only dramatic moments and deep discussions about trauma are the only way to establish close relationships. Trauma and scars are not prerequisites to becoming a close family, but often those scars prevent us from establishing and holding on to meaningful relationships.

If I learned anything through our pandemic hikes and could give any sort of advice, it would be this: spend time with your family and take the time to listen to what they have to say. Your life is important and you absolutely should be ambitious in pursuing your goals and aspirations, but there are more important things in life than achieving your goals and solving the conundrums of life, such as forging relationships with your family and your friends. Those relationships will be more valuable and rewarding than any achievement or award you will receive as you navigate your way through life.

My brother and I grew up in a religious household. My mother had always been a Christian and my father came to Christ in his early thirties. Even though my father was a baby Christian in every aspect, his desire to serve the church was stronger than that of most lifelong Christians. In June 2019, he accepted the position of youth pastor at our church. Since then, my brother and I have watched our father preach every Sunday. Even at the tender age of thirteen, I was proud of my father for preparing and delivering heartfelt sermons every week and desiring all members of our youth ministry to experience the joy he had in following Christ. Although I never fully understood some of the complex words he used and there were many times when the topics he discussed were too complicated for me to wrap my head around, I went home every Sunday with a warm feeling in my heart, grateful that God gave my father that opportunity.

When the pandemic came upon us in April 2020, our church, like all other churches throughout the world, had to reassess how we conducted worship on a short-term and a long-term basis. In the short term, we had to create a makeshift worship service in one week. In the long term, all gatherings and meetings, from church services to educational courses, would incorporate an online component. My father had to quickly adapt to conducting virtual worship services, and this was not easy. But this was not a burden that our family was going to let him bear by himself—our whole family was going to chip in and make this virtual church work. While the pandemic was difficult in so many ways, virtual worship was the most challenging obstacle for our family because none of us was particularly tech-savvy.

Immediately, we drowned ourselves in the world of YouTube DIY tutorials that showed viewers how to produce and record live-streamed services and upload pre recorded videos. We decided that the filming location would be our dining room, but we had to consider many other factors when it came to broadcasting the sermon to our congregation. First, we had to establish ideal lighting conditions. My mother purchased a specialized podcast lighting system from Amazon and my brother and I were in charge of setting it up. We also invested in a microphone because my father's voice was low and deep, which can come across as mumbling through a video. After our production crew prepared the studio for the sermon, my father would button up his collared shirt, slick back his hair with extra-strength hair gel, put on his basketball shorts, and sit down on the chair with an "X" marked on it. My mother was the de facto director and my brother and I stood by to do whatever was necessary to make the production run smoothly. Even though we got better and better at producing these videos, the struggle was always there for my brother and me to hold in our laughter as we were recording. We would be ten minutes into recording when the low battery signal flashed and then started to make beeping noises, at which point we would have to start all over again. Not only would my mother's hand start shaking from holding the camera (we went through multiple camera stands before finally finding the right one), she would also have to throw up hand signals to my father to tilt his head or adjust his body to fit into the recording frame. Sometimes, we would have done ten takes or so due to any number of mishaps, and by the third take, my father would be sweating profusely to the point of needing to change his shirt. This is how we spent the first nine Saturdays of the lockdown—at our dining room table, barely able to hold in our laughter as we prepared a prerecorded worship service. Through our collective efforts in recording these services, I found great joy and comfort in worshipping with my family in my home.

For the next ten services, we were actually able to go to church and live stream the service. The four of us conducted Sunday service with no one in the sanctuary but us. Because these services were live, there were no opportunities for multiple takes. Instead, we were producing a live event and the four of us took on that challenge as well. My father sang worship songs and preached, my mother handled the camera, my brother was in charge of the sound, and I controlled the lighting. We were not professionals by any stretch of the imagination and the production of the video and live service were probably comically bad, but I will never forget the memories we shared as a family in bringing it all to fruition in the tumultuous first few weeks of the pandemic. We had no idea how the pandemic would materialize or what church would be like five years from then, but our family came together to provide worship services for our youth ministry, and in the process we became a close-knit unit. I realized that doing the job well was important (our church would be watching us), but what was special for me was the memories we created through our teamwork and how we strengthened our relationships through this experience.

If I had to choose between having COVID-19 be a part of our lives or never having it ever invade our existence, I would choose to do without it one million times out of a million. But the moments I shared with my family because of the coronavirus are precious and I hold those memories close to my heart. At the end of the day, your family is your biggest cheerleader when the world can seem apathetic at best. They will lift you up with encouragement, but also build you up with bitter truths and honest rebukes. They will help you open your mind to achieve limitless possibilities and be that backbone of support for your goals and aspirations. COVID-19 showed me how valuable my time with my family is and how often we all overlook this simple fact.

I also realized how small of a window we have to enjoy the company of our families. In this sense, I am grateful that the pandemic shut down our busy lives and locked us up in our houses so that we could get to know each other and create an intimate bond with every family member. The pandemic has run its course, but it is not too late to rekindle these relationships with your loved ones. If there is one thing we learned through the shutdown, it is that you can have intimate conversations with someone on the other side of the planet through a wide variety of platforms on the Internet—take advantage of them! Enjoy a simple dinner with your family, relish the grocery store runs with your mother, reach out to those relatives in faraway places, but, most importantly, tell your family that you love them. Not only is our time on this earth short, but the time we have with our family is limited and the window is closing fast for all of us. Reach out now and start creating those memories because it is never too late to do so—I'm rooting for you!

DEAR BODY

From my earliest memories to the present day, eating has been and continues to be the greatest joy of my life. I looked forward to my summer breaks in South Korea every year because I could indulge in beef short ribs, Korean fried chicken, and cream-and-jam-covered waffles. My daily meal of choice in kindergarten was a bowl of rice mixed with two eggs with runny yolks, a tablespoon of soy sauce, and a tablespoon of sesame oil. As children, we want to fit in, and this mentality often causes us to avoid taking a foreign lunch to school—we would rather stick to something safe, like a sandwich. However, I was not ashamed to take traditional Korean food to school for lunch because it tasted better than the cafeteria food most of the time. It did not matter to me that my friends might tease me about how my lunch smelled or looked. I always put my own satisfaction above what others thought of me. I also loved to eat a variety of foods and have always had a reputation for eating everything on my plate. I was also a fast eater. When I would eat with my brother, he would work on finishing his meal and I was already thinking about dessert. Food had always made me happy and I could always depend on food to cheer me up when I felt sad or anxious, but it quickly became the source of my sadness, anger, and shame.

It never occurred to me that my body was different from that of other girls until we became members of a Korean church. I was eight years old when my family began attending a Korean church and I first became friends with Korean Americans. Like most Korean churches, the church our family attended served lunch after service. On Sunday mornings, I looked forward to the delicious meal that would be served more than the actual worship service. Before I knew it, the lunch ladies knew my name and gave me double portions because of the radiant smile I displayed when I was given what I desired. I enjoyed the food and I cherished those Sundays because I had no idea that I was heavy and I ate double and triple portions free of guilt. I had no idea of how people perceived me, and, even if I did, at that time I did not care—I just wanted to eat, and I wanted to eat big portions.

At ten years of age is when I started to become self-conscious about my body. As my family got more and more involved with the church, we were invited to many small-group fellowships and other gatherings at members' houses. At most of these gatherings, my friends were also there, and we always made the most out of the time we spent together. On one particular Sunday night, we all decided to go swimming, but I didn't have a swimsuit. My friend offered to let me and another friend borrow her extra swimsuits. The other friend put it on and was in the water. I headed to the restroom to put on the swimsuit and it was far too small. I did not want to believe that I couldn't fit into my friend's swimsuit. After all, we were the same height and age and in the same grade—I should have been able to fit in the swimsuit. I ended up having to wear her older sister's swimsuit, and I felt embarrassed. For the first time, I realized that I was heavier than the average girl my age.

From that point on, my insecurities about my body intensified and I mind-numbingly began comparing my body with those of my friends. I also began dreading my annual doctor's visit because I knew exactly what I was going to hear from her. It seemed pointless to go every year and have her tell me, "you're overweight and need to do something about it." I would hear this, feel awful about it, and go home that night and eat my heart out. Perhaps my mother felt bad for me after my annual exams, but she always seemed to prepare a meal fit for a queen on those days and I would gorge on dinner. I would then follow up my dinner with after-dinner snacks from our pantry, which was always stocked with my favorites. I would hope and pray that I would see an overweight doctor so that they could not tell me to lose weight, but even I knew at the age of eleven that that mindset was foolish and unreasonable. After every doctor's visit, I would lie to myself and my parents, saying that I would exercise and eat a healthy diet to lose weight, but it never happened. And I knew it never would. I had been obese my entire life, so it was difficult to picture myself thin and healthy. It was impossible to imagine myself as someone who exercises and eats healthy food, but it was even more inconceivable that I could be as thin and as beautiful as the girls in my Instagram feed. My parents were also probably resigned to the fact their daughter would carry her unhealthy eating habits into adulthood and that she would be overweight for the rest of her life. However, my doctor's visit around my twelfth birthday triggered something in my parents—something had to be done about my weight and my health. Not only did I fail the optics test and look significantly bigger than a year before, I was 20 pounds heavier, and I weighed significantly more than the average sixth grade girl. That is when my father decided that he would put me on a morning run regimen.

For whatever reason, 5:30 a.m. was the time when my father loved to begin physical activities as we did on our pandemic hikes, and he woke me every morning at that time to go on our runs. We would bang out two miles every morning, and I did not enjoy it at all. It did not matter to him that I had had loads of homework the night before and I ended up studying past my bedtime. He woke me up every morning at the crack of dawn and prioritized my health more than I did. I was never more jealous of my brother as I rubbed my eyes and changed into my running clothes, as he continued to sleep in his warm and cozy bed without ever having to worry about being woken up to the alarm clock that was my father's voice. I became accustomed to opening my eyes at 5:30 a.m., anticipating my father's footsteps as he walked into my room.

The first 500 meters were always the most painful because I had no breathing patterns and quickly developed cramps because I was not getting enough oxygen to my muscles. My calves were swollen for the rest of the day and my thighs rubbed against one another, creating burns between my inner legs. I remember having to apply baby powder and not being able to wear shorts to school for a week because of the severity of the chafing between my thighs. I was miserable because I could not achieve the high of exercising that most people constantly talked about and the whole experience of getting in shape only served to discourage me and did not motivate me to change my attitude about getting fit and healthy. I still had no desire to truly change my lifestyle. Our morning runs were more of a testament to my father's desire for his daughter to be healthy rather than my own motivation to change. When someone else wants something to happen for you more than you do, the results will never materialize because it is never your desire or aspiration. All of the self-help resources and well-meaning people you surround yourself with can do nothing to help you if your attitude and motivation do not change, and this was never more evident than it was for me at that season of my life. Although I ran two miles every morning at 5:30 with my father, my poor eating habits continued and I had no desire to change. I was not only deceiving myself about becoming healthy, but I was also not being entirely truthful to my father about giving my maximum effort to losing weight and getting into shape.

Seventh grade is when I discovered volleyball, and I instantly fell in love with that sport. I weighed in at 145 pounds and was 10 pounds heavier than a year before. As heavy as I was, I decided that I wanted to pursue volleyball seriously and asked my parents if I could try out for a competitive club volleyball team. I went into tryouts that year expecting to make it into one of the bottom-tier teams. Aside from the fact that I started volleyball later than the typical age, I was too heavy to quickly move my feet on the court like the rest of the girls. As I expected, I did not make it into one of the top tier teams and was selected onto the second-to-the-bottom team of that club. I was not disappointed to be in a bottom-tier team, as some of my teammates were, and I was determined to do my best with whatever role the coaches had for me. In fact, volleyball became secondary to the friendships I made with my teammates; so much so that I valued that over volleyball itself. It was not that I did not care for volleyball, but I was grateful for the new friends I made, some of whom I still keep in touch with to this day. It is possible that I was looking for acceptance from my peers at that age more than volleyball glory, which is what most seventh graders are seeking, and I found it with my teammates as we worked toward a common goal of winning volleyball matches. I was still overweight and I was still eating everything I wanted, but when I look back to that time of my life, I had never been happier because I was thriving in volleyball, in academics, and in my newly discovered social life.

Because I had found some success through my club volleyball team, I mustered up enough courage to try out for my school volleyball team and became the starting setter for my team. My school team was extra special because the teammates I became friends with were not just volleyball teammates but were classmates that I saw every day. I experienced a sense of belonging that was not restricted to the volleyball court but extended into the hallways of junior high with friends I saw on a daily basis. I am still friends with those teammates and we look back fondly to that time. I had found my comfort zone with my club team and my school team, and seventh grade was a year I look back on fondly with dear memories. The confidence and comfort I felt allowed me to take volleyball seriously and really put forth effort into perfecting my craft as the designated setter for both teams. My newly discovered motivation and hunger to become better at volleyball was especially rewarding because it bought me a ticket out of the 5:30 a.m. runs with my father. My father assured me that if I took volleyball seriously and took no shortcuts to my fitness through volleyball practices, he would consider allowing me a pass on our morning runs and I accepted the challenge gladly. I complained endlessly about our runs and the toll it was taking on my comfort, but in a strange way I did enjoy the time I spent with my father running into the dark abyss every morning. But I would rather get fit running drills for volleyball with my friends than run two miles mindlessly in the dark any day of the week, and it was a promise that I was not going to break with my father.

Volleyball saved my life by providing me with a pathway of enjoyable yet vigorous exercise. Our practices were no joke and our game schedule was grueling. We would run drills that left me drenched in sweat and exhausted beyond anything I experienced through a two-mile run. The games were scheduled for eight-hour tournaments on Saturdays and Sundays, exacting a toll not only on the players but on the parents as well. Through my newfound love of volleyball, I abandoned my previous sedentary lifestyle and transitioned into a more physically active life. I gave my maximum effort during drills and worked hard at perfecting my craft as a setter, absorbing as much of the coaching as I could and supplementing it with the vast resources available on the Internet. I had discovered an obsession, and it was volleyball! However, I could not escape that other little obsession called eating that was a thorn in my side even as I was hitting my stride as a starting setter for my club team.

This substantial transformation I was undergoing should have translated into a fit and lean volleyball-playing machine who shed all of her "baby fat," and there certainly was a noticeable difference in my attitude. Volleyball did bring about a fundamental change in my lifestyle and it contributed to an important period of change in my psyche, but I still was not able to completely discard the one weakness that had haunted me my entire life—food. I pushed myself to my physical limits until my legs gave out at every practice, but I consumed triple the number of calories I burned when I got home. I realized that I could use food as a reward for my hard work at practice and I continued to gain weight even as I was pouring my heart and soul out during practices. After practices, I would beg my mother to take me to Chipotle so I could treat myself to a 2-pound carne asada burrito. The two hours of excruciating cardio and scrimmaging went down the drain after every practice. A lot had changed in my mentality, but in many ways things remained the same when it came to my diet. The only difference was that this time, my unhealthy diet was cleverly masked by my achievements on the volleyball court.

By the season's end in May, I had improved significantly as the starting setter and had gained the respect and trust of my coaches and teammates. At the yearly team banquet, I was recognized as the "Most Improved Player" on the team and I basked in the glory of my volleyball prowess. I was proud of myself not only in terms of what I had accomplished on the volleyball court, but for the friendships I had made that year. I have nothing but fond memories of that school year and I can state unequivocally that it was the best year of my short life. I had good grades, I was killing it in volleyball, and I had a group of friends who I could relate to and could have fun with. On top of that, I was able to spend a month in Hawaii with my family before I came back to doing what I enjoyed more than anything at that time—volleyball.

I came back home from Hawaii with a renewed sense of desire to take my game to the next level. I attended every summer league opportunity my volleyball club offered. I knew that I had to work twice as hard as the other girls to become noticed by the coaches during tryouts because I was not the most fit or the most talented. I tried to make up for my slow agility by speaking up on the court, picking up the volleyballs when no one else wanted to, and encouraging my teammates with a smile and a pat on the back. All of this hard work in the summer seemed to have paid off because by a miraculous twist of fate, I was able to secure a spot on the second-highest team of my club along with a few of my friends from the previous season. I made the under-fourteen national team and felt ecstatic. Making this team was special in many respects, but mostly because it would entail traveling out of the state for competition with my closest friends. The excitement of traveling with my teammates to compete was intoxicating and it filled me with joy and anticipation, not to mention that my volleyball acumen was being recognized by the powers that be. The news of my selection was a cause for celebration for my family and we commemorated it accordingly. That night, my father did what he did best—he cooked the family special of rib eye steaks stuffed with garlic cloves, grilled asparagus, and grilled onions. I was proud of my accomplishments and I feasted sumptuously and was on cloud nine the rest of the weekend.

As the season kicked off, I began experiencing a competitive spirit within the team. I was one of two setters on the team, and I experienced constant comparison throughout the entire season. I understood it was like that for any position in volleyball and for any sport in general, but it was an awful feeling that led me to display a false sense of camaraderie with my teammates, but especially so with the other setter. I had always been a blunt child who had no trouble speaking my mind. I think that's why it was difficult for me to balance my feelings of jealousy and competitiveness on and off the court.

While all of my teammates were friends, we still had cliques within the team with whom we would discuss our true feelings about the coaches and other teammates. As toxic as it may sound, that is what happens when you get a bunch of teenage girls together. We were a team aspiring to win the same game, yet our competitiveness and our desire to be the best ultimately trickled into how we played the game. I always harbored this feeling that my teammates, my coaches, my teammates' parents, and even the general audience were always comparing me with the other setter. For the first time in my short volleyball career, my mental health began to spiral negatively and I felt like I was losing control of my mental faculties. I often felt the pressure of having to live up to my coaches' and my own expectations. The other setter was more experienced than I was and I was scared to death of my underdog status on the team. I became obsessed with every minutia of how my competitor moved and went about her practice routine. This was not good for my mental health and this did not improve my performance on the court, but I still chose to compare myself to her because deep down I knew that she was the better setter.

At first, it was only her volleyball skills that I tried to emulate, but I quickly began to compare our bodies. I began to fall into the reckless cycle that most women sadly experience to some degree, the starving and binging cycle. I starved myself and was thrilled to see my body weight dropping significantly, but that also led me to binge on junk food the next day. I would suffocate myself with healthy and unhealthy food even when I felt satiated. I recall one of my friends asking me halfway through the year why I stopped bringing lunch to school. It was because I looked at school as the perfect way to skip two meals of my day, but when I got home, I lost my ability to control

24

my appetite. The exhaustion that came with living up to unreasonable standards of body type (most of which were in my head) became unbearable. I had developed an eating disorder without knowing it, and my body could not keep up with the sudden changes I was making to my eating habits. I went to bed on countless nights sobbing about my body. I skipped countless family dinners because I knew that my weight would go up the next morning if I indulged in that meal. I canceled countless hangouts because my weight was not where it was "supposed to be." I had to shop for clothes in the women's section because no sizes for my age fit me. The sad truth is that there are so many women who go through the same experiences as I did, some at an even younger age and with more severe consequences. As a society, we tend to overlook eating disorders, and my experience with body dysmorphia through my participation in club volleyball showed me how detrimental eating disorders can be to mental and physical health.

As time passed, volleyball became a chore rather than a hobby for me. Coach J, my club coach in the eighth grade, was unlike any previous coach I had—she was a harsh coach with a loving heart. It seemed to me that my mother would drive an hour not to drop me off at volleyball practice, but for me to get rebuked by Coach J for the same mistakes over and over again. I began going to practice expecting my coach to yell at and belittle me. I dreaded going to practice because I knew what the coach would criticize me for before I even stepped foot on the court. While my school life was manageable, my love for volleyball faded and even the amazing friendships I had on the team were not enough to soothe the lack of confidence I had on the court. My poor eating habits continued to worsen and at the age of thirteen, I had no idea how to handle my emotions. All of these feelings continued until the night of January 9, 2020.

I attended practice that night with the same deficient mindset and anticipated that that night would play out like all of the previous practices we had. That particular practice was one of the worst practices I had to endure. I could not move my feet quickly enough, so I continued to let balls drop on the court and none of my sets were heading in the right direction. I was all over the place and the entire team knew it. It was the one time that I was at my absolute worst and my competitor was hitting on all cylinders and nailing every set. I had planned to distance myself from my teammates and coaches even before practice began and those feelings just intensified as the practice was winding down. I didn't want to socialize after practice nor did I want to stay after practice to work on my craft further, which was what I usually did. There was nothing I wanted to do more than to escape and go home. However, after those two hours of being mentally and physically drained, there was a sharp feeling in my chest that I knew would get worse if I had stuck with my original plan. As lousy a practice as it had been, I had to talk to Coach J about what I was feeling and I had to get my frustrations off my chest.

I have always struggled with expressing my feelings to others. A big part of this struggle was due to my fear of making myself vulnerable enough to share those feelings. Another fear that crippled me was that people would pity me, and I did not want that at all. It petrified me to no end to muster up enough courage to approach Coach J to talk to her about my recent performance on the court. It did not help that she naturally had a stern look on her face that intimidated me and my teammates. I repeatedly pushed the cuticles of my fingers back as a means to stop myself from shedding tears in front of her. I had always believed that tears were a sign of weakness and I could not dare to expose my weakness to Coach J, especially since I was going to confront her about my performance and her harshness in dealing with me. I made my way toward her and immediately felt a rush of anger and sadness flooding my veins. I promised myself moments before approaching her that I would not get emotional, but at that very moment my chest coiled up and my heart raced faster than ever. When I approached her to vent, our conversation proceeded as I thought it would and Coach J unloaded on me relentlessly.

She told me that I was an uncoachable player and that I moved in slow motion on the court. The one thing Coach J said that I will never forget was this: "You don't move your feet." I can vividly remember her saying this to me like it happened yesterday—her authoritative tone, the salty tears dripping down into the corners of my mouth, the feeling of my chest tightening up from my effort to suppress my emotions. It was not necessarily the words that she said that upset me that night, but it was the fact that I knew from the beginning of the season that everything she said was true.

My dad was waiting for me in the parking lot as I came out of the facility with a solemn look on my face. I flung open the door of his car and immediately burst into tears. He asked me what had happened and I told him everything without sugarcoating any of the events that transpired. I told him the blatant truth, fully expecting him to take my side and console me. I was instead bombarded with the same relentless rebuke I had just endured from Coach J. It felt as if Coach J was driving me home and I was being labeled "uncoachable" all over again. Both my coach and my father told me things I did not want to hear and that I deliberately tried to avoid in my head. I could not run from the truth for the first time in my life: I was stubborn and I abhorred the advice of my coaches and my parents. I had always known in the back of my head what my issues were and could have gotten away with forgetting about them without ever feeling badly about myself. However, now that two people whom I respected very much were telling me these things, I knew there was no escaping my problems. I had to change if I wanted to enjoy volleyball again and live a healthy and productive life.

When we arrived at home, my mother and my brother were at the dinner table. She prepared dinner for the four of us to eat as a family, but I clearly wasn't interested in eating that night. By that time, my mother had gotten pretty good at assessing my mood after practice. When I was in a good mood, I came through the door singing a song that was stuck in my head or I immediately shouted, "I'm home!" When I was not feeling my best, I stayed silent and headed straight to my room, which was exactly what I did that night. My father explained to her what had happened at practice. I did not come out of my room and did not even bother to greet my mother or my brother, even though I had not seen them all day. My eyes were puffy and I looked like a mess because I cried the entire drive home. As I sat there crying, my father eventually called me out of my room to come have a talk. I was already tired and was not in the mood to talk to anyone for the rest of the night, but I was forced to explain to my mother what had happened without leaving out any details.

Through this experience of talking to my mother, I was reminded of her greatest quality—she always listened to my side of the story and she never made any assumptions. She always tried to understand where I was coming from before she made any judgments about my actions, whether I was right or wrong. After she listened to what I had to say, she asked me if I wanted to go on a walk with her. My initial inclination was to decline because I was tired and worn out from the night. However, a sudden wave of optimism came over me and I thought that expressing my feelings further to my mother would be much more effective than having a discourse with my father. I loved my father and I took to heart what he said in the car, but in that moment I knew that I would only get riled up if I continued to hear the things that were making me writhe in emotional pain. My mother, on the other hand, had a way with words and could say that you were absolutely wrong about something in the nicest and most compelling way possible. I put on my sneakers and went outside with my mother late at night.

In those forty-five minutes of brisk sauntering, my mother gave me the hope that I needed to achieve my goals successfully. She built me up and encouraged me to take accomplishing my goals one step at a time. I felt the tenseness in my chest gradually dissipate. Talking about my feelings with my mother alleviated the stress I had been feeling since the season started and I was grateful that my mother took the time to listen to what was on my mind. When I got home from the walk that night I was feeling more motivated than ever to improve my lifestyle in a sustainable and healthy way. I finally had a fire lit inside of me to want to become better and healthier. I was sick and tired of feeling miserable in my own body and I was exasperated at not being able to do anything about it. I did not want to give Coach J any more ammunition to ever call me uncoachable again, so I decided to stay committed to the team and the remaining season. I decided to hold myself accountable and vowed to do anything necessary to become the best version of myself.

Complacency is one of the most dangerous states of existence in which anyone can find themselves. I was far too comfortable with my destructive lifestyle until I endured one of the worst practices of my life. I recently shared this experience with one of my close friends and why it occupies such a sentimental place in my heart. My friend, as any good friend would do, took my side and told me that my coach was way too harsh on a thirteen-year-old teenage girl. However, I now appreciate what Coach J told me that night because if she hadn't, I do not think I would have fostered a desire to truly change my lifestyle. I am certain that if I had not endured that one terrible practice, my mental and physical health would have continued to degenerate at the pace it was going. Thankfully, I was able to break free from my state of complacency and act positively toward achieving my goals. January 9, 2020, was the last time I gorged on junk food. I began packing homemade healthy meals for lunch and continued to attend volleyball practice, but going forward I practiced with a different mindset. I promised myself that I would try my absolute hardest on the court even when I was dealt harsh criticisms. I absorbed every bit of what my coaches told me to work on and started practicing those same skills in my backyard at home. While my father was doing his workouts on the heavy bag in our backyard, I set the ball against the wall from various distances and ran sprints on the pavement. I began feeling a sense of peace with my new mindset of tackling whatever obstacles stood in my way, but it was a lesson on patience as I did not notice drastic differences in my skills on the court. I expected instantaneous changes, but I learned that change happens gradually and that I have to keep chipping away at the negativity to build it into positivity. I was also going to learn that life often throws curveballs at you and that lessons you learn in one arena of life are not always for that arena, but they are frequently utilized and maximized in a completely different area of life that you could never have imagined.

We were gearing up for the home stretch of the season. We were looking forward to our season-ending tournament in April 2020 at Las Vegas, Nevada, and had already booked airline tickets and hotel accommodations for the weeklong competition. I was making steady progress and becoming the coachable player that Coach J had wanted. Just as all of this was materializing, an unprecedented worldwide phenomenon broke out that we came to know as the COVID-19 pandemic. The coronavirus not only put an abrupt end to our season, but it brought the entire world to a screeching halt. Arizona was shut down toward the end of March, ending our volleyball season and effectively ending in-person schools as well. I had put so much effort into becoming a great volleyball player and had endured so much from Coach J to get to where I was, and the culmination of my efforts was essentially wiped out single-handedly by a virus that we could not even see. My past self would have lashed out in anger and wallowed in sorrow, but I had made major character adjustments and was prepared for whatever obstacles that lay ahead. The path that I had mapped out that season was to volleyball glory, but my journey was just beginning, and that journey was not going to involve volleyball at all. The lessons I learned and the hardships I encountered, however, were blessings that I was going to carry with me on this wonderful new adventure.

The shutdown of schools and all nonessential activities happened immediately after our spring break, and this included all in-person athletic activities. Volleyball clubs were no longer allowed to conduct practices in their facilities and I had to adapt to recording videos of myself practicing drills and posting them online for my coaches to see. Like most everyone around the world, I was expecting the lockdown to last two weeks at most, but the virus kept spreading at a rapid rate and we all came to realize that this lockdown would last much longer than a few weeks. I thought about how I had promised myself that I would accomplish all of my goals after that January night, yet I had not implemented any of them in my life. However, I realized that even though volleyball was taken away from me, it did not mean that I could go back to my old ways and forget about all the emotions I felt about what Coach J said to me. Her words resonated with me and I still desired to get better at setting so I could make her eat her words. I wanted to show her that I was coachable, yet somehow I had a feeling that volleyball was in the rearview mirror. Instead, I viewed the pandemic lockdown as the perfect opportunity for me to reorganize the personal goals I had made for myself at the beginning of the year. Time was no longer an excuse, for I had all the time in the world to do anything I wanted while I was stuck in quarantine. There truly was no excuse that could hinder me from getting in shape this time.

Since I could no longer rely on volleyball practices as my source of exercise, I looked to high-intensity interval training (HIIT) workouts. I laid out my mother's yoga mat, put on my indoor running shoes, and exercised in the living room every day. These workouts were intense and challenged my mind and my body in a way reminiscent of volleyball practices. After every HIIT workout, I was pleasantly surprised by the puddle of sweat I left on the floor. My legs trembled after each vigorous session and my body throbbed from the intensity of the workouts. When each workout concluded, my shirt was always drenched in sweat and I began to feel that high that people talk about. I had left volleyball behind and I had begun my love affair with fitness without even knowing it, and exercising quickly became a necessary part of my life.

Since most restaurants were shut down during COVID, I could not eat out as much as I did before. I had no choice but to cook my own meals and take control of what I was putting into my body. It was during this time I developed my love for cooking and baking and chose to eat a healthier diet. I had this preconception that healthy food only consisted of salads and that I had to cut out carbohydrates, but this was a complete fallacy. Many influencers online had fit bodies yet also consumed pancakes, brownies, cookies, etc. As I watched more YouTube videos to fulfill my curiosity about dieting, I learned that I had failed to control my weight because I had restricted myself from eating the food I enjoy and because I made a mental list of "good" and "bad" foods. This was a shocking revelation and I wish I had known this sooner. Beginning when I was a child, well-meaning adults would make casual rude comments such as "eat a salad" or "eat less," and I came to believe that this was what I had to do to become thinner. After learning that I did not have to completely cut off the foods that I loved, I felt more optimistic about losing weight. I had the exercising part down—now it was time to fix my diet in a correct and sensible way.

Getting groceries during the pandemic was a huge hassle for my mother and father, as it was for everyone else. Watching them gear up in gloves and masks was like watching two soldiers prepare to go into battle. We had to limit the number of people going to the grocery store because of how chaotic it was to even be granted permission to enter the building. There was a list of things you had to do in order to safely shop at the store. Despite all of this, I still chose to tag along with my parents and they gladly welcomed me to go grocery shopping with them. I made the deliberate decision to select my own food so that I could extend the practice of self-control I had developed with my eating habits. I chose the ingredients that I would use to make the recipes I found on YouTube.

My parents were shocked the first time I went shopping with them. I had always reached for the Pop-Tarts or the Creamsicles when I was at the market, but I was putting things like fruits and vegetables into the basket—something that only my parents did. I made tasty yet nutritious meals and snacks for myself, and it didn't take long for me to fall in love with prepping my own meals. I consistently banged out the HIIT workouts at home, forced my family to go hiking with me on the weekends, and ate nourishing and delicious food for four consecutive months. Before I knew it, I had lost 20 pounds! I never even realized that I was losing weight during those four months because no one was there to recognize my weight loss due to the lockdown.

Since my family saw me every hour of the day, they could not see the dramatic change in my body. The clothes buried deep in my closet that had strangled me to the point of oxygen deprivation four short months earlier magically became loose on me. My fingers shrank in size and my ankles were no longer swollen. I could move my body around more freely and I wasn't as out of breath as I was before. For my birthday on July 17, 2020, my parents bought me my first pair of Air Jordans. I had wanted Air Jordans since the seventh grade but gave up on asking my parents for them because of how expensive they were. I was thrilled to see them in the shoebox and could not believe that what I had wanted so badly was right in front of me. When I put them on, I immediately wanted to put on an outfit and take birthday pictures outside. My family knew about my struggles to find an outfit to wear that would fit and be comfortable because most of them were too small. But I had a new and inconceivable problem—for the first time, I had nothing to wear because my clothes were too big! I had nothing to wear to match my new shoes because nothing in my closet fit! I had to buy new clothes, but that pesky little thing called COVID-19 put a wrinkle in shopping for clothes.

We did not have the opportunity to go shopping for new clothes after my weight loss because of COVID, so I resorted to online shopping. I was never able to enjoy the thrill of buying new clothes whether it was in person or online. I dreaded going to the mall because I knew that I would always come up empty—none of the clothes I wanted fit me. However, because of my newfound persona, I savored every moment of online shopping during the lockdown. I had trouble shopping online because I never really paid attention to what my size was prior to my weight loss. I had always bought clothes in the biggest size available or I chose to purchase baggy shirts and hoodies. I couldn't tell you what the size difference was from before and after the weight loss, but I knew clearly that my waist size was finally where it should have been. I had my mother bring out the measuring tape to measure my waist and hip size and I was finally able to buy new jeans for myself.

After shopping and making multiple purchases online, I threw on my mom's flannel and high school shorts and posed for pictures in front of the beautiful landscape of my front yard. I posted those pictures on my social media platforms and sat in my bed that night reading all of the comments people left under my post. Through this, I was exposed to a whole other side of social media that I never knew about. I could see why so many influencers were locked into their phones and so concerned about what their followers had to say about them. I repeatedly stared at the comments about how different I looked and how I looked healthier and happier since the COVID-19 outbreak. I felt amazing. The fact that many people were noticing the hard work that I put into getting in shape made me feel proud and made me think it was worth every hardship. I was the lightest I had been since fifth grade and I was at a healthy weight for my age. At 125 pounds, I started to live with the mindset that I was going to maintain this healthy lifestyle.

While losing weight and looking healthier is great for anyone who has struggled with obesity in some form, what is frequently not discussed is what happens after the initial weight loss, what I would refer to as the "post-weight-loss period." This period of sustaining my new weight turned out to be more difficult than I imagined and required more grit than it took for me to lose weight. Maintaining weight loss is the hardest part, and this is where most people go back to their normal ways. I knew that I would not be able to live with myself if I gained back the weight that I lost. I didn't want to go back to the life I had previously lived; I hated myself and I hated my body so much. I felt lucky that fear of becoming complacent again kept me in line. However, good things always seem to be accompanied by bad.

My workouts didn't change—I continued to work out to the point of exhaustion and until my legs were trembling. On the other hand, I began to fall back to some bad eating habits again. I would chug water bottles before meals so that I wouldn't be hungry and when I was hungry, I would starve myself because of the fear that I would revert to the person I used to be. I tricked myself into thinking that I was intermittently fasting from 12:00 p.m. to 8:00 p.m. But the reality was that I would starve myself until 9:00 p.m., at which point I would eat everything I saw in the pantry. It seemed as if the vicious cycle of starving and binging never left me but was kept dormant for a period before it reared its ugly head after a period of triumph. I felt like I was alive but barely breathing. Food became my biggest enemy again and when I couldn't resist binging, I punished myself with hours of intense cardio and extreme weightlifting. The only difference between then and before was that self-loathing had been replaced by the punishment I was inflicting on myself through the intense workout sessions.

My knowledge of fitness and nutrition was still infantile, so I was fixated on the mindset that I had to burn every calorie I took in. This took a tremendous toll on my psyche as I spent an enormous amount of time calculating calories, most of the time incorrectly. Everything in my life revolved around my weight and if it went up even by a fifth of a pound, I panicked. Weighing myself every morning became the ticking time bomb in my family—would it explode or would we make it through another day? When my weight was where it was "supposed" to be, I came out of my room in a jolly mood and was energetic to start the day. When my weight was even a little bit over what it should have been, I broke down in tears and made everyone uncomfortable. Seeing the numbers on the scale go up was heart-wrenching for me and it only meant one thing—I would have to starve myself for that day.

When I look back now, it is hard to rationalize my behavior regarding my weight. However, I think the reason for my irrational behavior after weighing myself was not because of my actual weight, but because I didn't know if I would have the perseverance and the strength to starve myself the entire day. The self-control required to starve myself the entire day broke me down to the point of exhaustion and a sense of hopelessness paralyzed me to the core. I couldn't focus on anything I was doing, whether that was doing my homework or working out in my backyard. My singular focus on getting healthy had sustained me in getting me there, but my efforts to maintain my healthier position propelled me to starve my body of nutrition and caused me to feel depressed and exhausted.

This season of my life was very difficult and it transpired during the heart of the pandemic. While I cannot profess to know what everyone was going through as the coronavirus was ravaging all of our lives, I can certainly empathize with the hardships we all had to endure within the confines of our own homes with very little support or contact with others outside of the household. For me, my family was there to encourage me in my ordeals. However, I cannot deny that the isolation from friends and extended family members took a toll on my coping abilities. I can only imagine how difficult it might have been for people dealing with more serious matters of life and death during the pandemic—I feel heartbroken about those experiences and hope that those stories will also be told to the world.

My weight loss journey in itself could be a topic for another book, but my intent is not to simply chronicle an anecdote of weight loss and healthy living. I am not the first person to discover that fitness and a sensible diet can lead to a healthy lifestyle. However, by sharing a small portion of my past life I hope that someone who is struggling with those same demons will realize that they are not alone and they do not have to be a slave to their eating disorder. It is so important to be mindful that major changes take time. If you are struggling with an eating disorder, you cannot overcome those struggles overnight—it is impossible. I believed that I had conquered my demons when I shed 20 pounds in four months. I had won the initial battle, but the war to obtain healthy living had just begun and I was challenged to sustain my newfound lifestyle. But the biggest challenge for me was not the emotional toil or the physical strain, but simple ignorance.

I never acknowledged my eating disorder when it appeared because I was young and did not even know what that was. My parents were always supportive of everything I did, but they were also fighting a battle that they knew little about. The sad truth is that most of our difficulties with eating arise at an early age, just as they did for me. I was labeled the "shy fat girl" in middle school and was always picked last for games and teams. I was constantly putting myself on diets at that young age and felt so out of place wherever I was. I made sure to make fun of myself before others could, and I used laughter as a way to hide the true pain I felt. For some of you reading this book, these scenarios are all relatable to you. For some of you, your heart hurts reading this because it takes you back to how worthless and shameful you felt about yourself and how others made you feel. Even today, I still struggle with eating and exercising. However, the difference between how I battled my eating disorder during the height of the pandemic and how I am tackling it now is the people in my life. Those people were there then as they are now—my parents, my friends, and my mentors. They are here to check on me and pick me up when I stumble, but they are able to do this because I have reached out to them and have invited them into my life. No one on the face of this earth hates seeking help more than me. To humbly make yourself vulnerable and seek help is hard and goes against the natural tendency to erect a wall of bravado for protection, but we cannot do the things we desire by ourselves. When I invited the people I trusted into my life's struggles, I felt an overwhelming sense of relief that I was not fighting this war by myself. The stress and the pain of this struggle did not disappear, but they were instantly alleviated because I had someone to turn to.

Seeking help, whether it be from your friends, your family, or even a teacher you are close with at school, can make the biggest difference in how you view the challenges you face in life, as well as how you go about dealing with those challenges. Life is built on friendships and we as humans are meant to connect with one another on deeper levels—that is God's original design for us as stated in 1 Thessalonians 5:11: "Therefore encourage one another and build one another up, just as you are doing." What may seem unbearable at that moment can be turned into a seed of optimism and faith through what may seem like an insignificant conversation with someone. One random FaceTime call can be the one conversation that will change your life. My complicated relationship with food and my body started before I even understood what it meant to love myself. My entire life was devoted to breathing, existing, and losing weight, and those wounds still affect me today. Those physical and mental scars are what make me who I am. My physical transformation is what people noticed first, but it could not have happened without the change of my heart and mind. The inner part of me had to change first, or I would not have cared to even fix the outer parts of myself. Those five years of constantly feeling pity, sorrow, depression, and uselessness were imprinted into my brain for a long time. I had resigned myself to being the "fat girl" for the rest of my life and I accepted that I would never obtain my "dream body." While the insecurities will never go away, the physical changes did come about when I stopped feeling sorry for myself and stopped making my long list of excuses. Actor Robert Urich once said that a healthy outside starts from the inside. When you approach change from the inside out, you gain a strong sense of worthiness and capability you cannot feel when you live from the outside in. I encourage all of you to seek this inside-out change!

YOU WILL FIND YOUR PEOPLE

Finding a group of friends in junior high and high school was always difficult for me. There were many reasons for this, but the primary reason was that I had trouble trusting people. This lack of ability to trust probably was a result of my being an extreme introvert. It also did not help that I changed school districts between sixth and seventh grade and between eighth grade and high school. Despite my struggles, I was able to find a group of friends toward the end of sixth grade. I still keep in touch with these friends, but most of my junior high friends ended up going to different high schools. This transition from junior high to high school, which is as difficult a transition as there is, was made all the more bewildering because of the pandemic.

I had always thought that freshman year was going to be the hardest year for me until I entered my sophomore year. Sophomore year was particularly difficult for me because it served as my first year actually on campus due to the pandemic interrupting my freshman year experience. As a freshman in high school in the midst of COVID-19, I woke up exactly two minutes before school started and attended school from the comfort of my own bed. I didn't have to get ready or put on clothes; I just turned my camera off and listened to the lecture. Good grades were not hard to maintain, for the workload was equivalent to the workload for a kindergartener. When I look back at my freshman year, I vividly remember the comfort and ease I felt while "going" to school, but I don't remember the many friendships I should have made, the football games I should have attended, and the various clubs I should have joined. I can jokingly say that I envy my brother for being able to experience all of those things during his freshman year. What every previous generation of eighth graders for the past 200 years or so took for granted, my generation was not able to experience. I wish that I had participated in all of the mundane things every freshman had partaken in, but this was not to be. We in the class of 2024 had our first year of high school taken away, but it made our sophomore year that much more special and precious. Not having a true freshman year under my belt turned out to be a positive experience because it allowed me to be even more grateful for the wonderful friendships I have made the past two years.

I have always valued reliable people. This is why I placed such importance on the reliability of friends when I searched for my friend group, but developing these friendships requires a lot of trust, trials, and tribulations. Because I had always struggled to make friends, my sophomore year of high school was one of the most difficult periods of my life. I had just learned to deal with my weight issues, but I found a new challenge as I entered high school. I had just one friend, and she was a friend from junior high. Like I mentioned before, sophomore year was one of the lowest points of my life. I thank God for putting her in my life because without her, I think my sophomore year would have been a lot more difficult. We didn't have any friends besides each other, but that allowed us to share a close bond that I had with no other person.

However, even with my junior high friend in my life, I still felt a pang of loneliness every time I stepped foot on campus. Walking around the halls, I saw how joyful the boys and girls were with their group of friends and I envied them. I didn't think that it was wrong for me to desire the large friend group that everyone else had—it was what every teenager wanted. As I entered my junior year, I promised myself that things would be different. I needed to expand my group of friends; I could not survive with one friend for yet another year of high school. On my first day of school in my math class, I sat at a random table, not knowing that the group of people at that table would become my closest friends. In my other classes, I made the effort to talk to new people and get to know them. I joined numerous clubs that interested me and even started one of my own. Through all of this, I built strong friendships that I never had the year before and I learned to enjoy high school the proper way, with friends. Within the first two months of school, I became extremely comfortable with my new friends and felt a sense of belonging when I was around them.

My church friends were like sisters to me. I had known them for more than half of my life, and we were all very close to one other. We were the same group of five girls from six years before, but I ended up growing apart from that group. I found another group of friends that I related to more closely as we hung out together more. My two new friends always struck me as intimidating yet they seemed so cool. So, when I was accepted into their friend group, I felt that this was a big opportunity for me and I could not mess this up. As much as I cherished every moment with them, I cannot say that the memories we created together were godly and went with the values of the Christian life I was pursuing before I began hanging out with them.

As a Christian and a pastor's daughter all my life, I knew that the way I behaved was being monitored by all church members and that I had to set an example for my peers. However, I found myself becoming more and more careless about my language, actions, and behavior when I became friends with these new girls. I did things that I never did before and I participated in doing things that my younger self would have scorned. This friendship was like a drug. The more I hung out with them, the more time I wanted to spend with them. The riskier our activities became, such as visiting shady neighborhoods and meeting shady people, the more lies I had to tell my parents just to hang out with them.

I was eventually introduced to their other friends who were not Korean American or religious, and this only enhanced the great times we had together. I would drive an hour every weekend across the city just to go to parties and indulge in stupid high school behavior with them. There were some weeks when I would spend both Saturday and Sunday with them just for a short-lived hangout, and I would return to school on Monday feeling drowsy and fatigued from how late I stood out the nights before. I fell asleep during lectures and my grades were declining, but when the weekend came, I was always ready to go out. There was always room for having fun—I made sure of it.

One of the events that made me realize that I was associating with the wrong group was when one of my friends got high during a church service. It was a Sunday afternoon and my father was preaching as usual. My friends told me that we would be sitting in the very back row that day because one of them was under the influence and she didn't want to be noticed. I immediately felt an intense tightness in my chest and an overwhelming sense of shame. My father was working hard for God's kingdom, preaching a sermon to the rest of the youth about how to live a godly life, yet here I was sitting next to my friend who was high and couldn't even think straight. Even atheists would acknowledge that being high for a church service is morally repugnant, which is why I felt devastated that my friend who had grown up in a Christian household was high for Sunday service. This was one of the first signs that I should distance myself from them, but I ignored these signs and continued to count them as my friends.

I maintained a good relationship with my junior high friend, and we even had a few classes together that year. In my AP US history class, I quickly became friends with two other people whom I will refer to as my high school friends. They had been close friends before I met them, but they welcomed me into their group. Their sense of humor instantly clicked with mine, which is why we got along so well. They were smart, caring, and authentic. However, they noticed a change in me as I started to hang out with my church trio more often. My new high school friends and I FaceTimed almost every night and we would talk for hours about the things going on outside of our school lives. I remember telling them the details of what my other two friends and I would do together, hoping to get a laugh out of them. They did not laugh and instead responded with heavy rebukes. They were showing me my blind spots, but I refused to see them as true friends who were only looking out for me. They were not judging me for my actions, but they could see that my other friends were a bad influence on me. This bad influence trickled into damaging my other relationships as well. It wasn't just my relationship with God that was in shambles because of this friendship, but my relationship with my family was becoming more distant as well.

My parents noticed a change in my mood and behavior when I spent time with these friends. This was first evident when I tried to be funny in front of my friend, so I disrespected my mother. It sounds foolish, right? Without even realizing it, I hurt my mom's feelings that night. As soon as my friend left my house, my father rebuked me and talked some sense into me about showing respect to my parents. However, I did not see this as a big deal and took his "lecture" very lightly. Once again, I ignored the signs that I should consider taking a break from them.

My close friends and family were not the only people who noticed my detrimental behavior. Casual acquaintances also noticed I was deliberately trying to change myself to be accepted by this friend group, but I refused to see what they saw. Despite the downward slope I was on through this friend-ship, I can say with complete confidence that God put these two friends in my life for a reason and always had a purpose for what I was going through. The spiritual battles I was experiencing were all a part of God's plan to create a firm foundation in me. God often allows us to face trials and tribulations in order to bring us closer to him, and I believe that is exactly what he did for me through my friends.

Even with every sinful act I committed and every wrongdoing I was a part of, I had always felt that God was there with me through it all, protecting me from the worst that could have happened to me. In March 2023, during my spring break, my parents and my brother went to California for my brother's rowing tournament. I was left home alone for the first time and my parents trusted that I would take care of the house and our newly adopted puppy. I cannot say what got into me, but I believe I completely lost my mind when I decided to throw a party. Perhaps I wanted to be accepted by my friends, or I wanted to be the cool teenager who could host a party. Whatever the case, I put my amateur party hat on and proceeded to plan this party weeks before my parents even left for California.

I asked my two friends to come a bit earlier to my house to help me properly set up the party. I knew that they were more experienced with this kind of stuff and had been to a lot more parties than I had, so I put this in their hands. When the clock hit 9:00 p.m., a lot of my school friends started to show up. There were around ten to fifteen people from school in my house, as well as my two friends. According to some of my friends, this was still too small of a number of people to be considered a party, so one of my school friends decided to post my address and gate code on her Snapchat account. Given that it was a Saturday night and spring break had just started, a lot more people started showing up to my house, most of whom I did not know and went to different schools. What happened in the next few hours proved to me how easy it was to have a situation spiral out of control.

At 4:00 a.m., I was asleep in my parents' master bedroom and had no idea what my friends were up to. The lights suddenly came on and when I opened my eyes, a tall Spanish man I had never seen in my life stood before me. He woke me up vigorously and repeated two words to me: "Cops downstairs! Cops downstairs!" A thousand thoughts ran through my head and I kept thinking to myself that this was a bad dream. I ran downstairs and was immediately greeted by many cops and firefighters sitting on my couch. I saw my two friends from school sitting on the couch with them and I felt so confused. Many people had already left by this time, but there were still a good number of people who had plans to spend the night at my house. They were all in our kitchen, some of whom were scrambling to leave before they would have to provide answers to the police about what was happening. There were police cars outside of my house, lined up one by one, and the cherry on top was the fire engine parked in our driveway. This was a scene out of a movie that I could not have written even if I had the creative juices to do so. My stomach began to turn when I thought about what I had done to create such a scene.

I asked a friend what had happened and she told me that one of my other friends had consumed a large number of marijuana edibles and had "greened out," a term that referred to a marijuana overdose. Another one of my friends, who was with the girl who took the edibles, saw how her eyes rolled back into her sockets and began having what appeared to be seizures on the floor. At this point, she called 911. After listening to what had happened, I immediately went to the kitchen table and saw bottles of alcohol everywhere. My house was a mess; the tables were sticky from the alcohol, the guest bathroom reeked of marijuana smoke, and cigarette butts were everywhere in my pool. One of the police officers asked me to call my mother, at which point my heart sank into my stomach. I knew how disappointed she would be and how I had completely broken her and my father's trust in me. Hearing my mother's voice at 4:30 a.m. allowed me to feel a type of shame that I had never felt before. My exact words to her, which I cannot remember because everything was hazy and unreal, were recounted to me by my parents later on: "Mommy, I think I am in trouble."

I struggled to find the words to explain what had happened as the police officers were yelling orders in the background to the few friends who remained throughout this whole ordeal. I was expecting my mother to start yelling at me and give me a long lecture about how I had just ruined my life by throwing this party, but she embraced me on the phone and told me to calm down, comforting me during this time of chaos and disorder. I had screwed up royally and felt like a complete loser. I saw my life flash before my eyes and began to envision doing time in prison for distributing drugs and overseeing the death of an innocent teenager due to overdose. I had ruined not only my life, but also the reputation of my parents.

When I look back at this event, I think it is a miracle I did not face any legal repercussions. The police very easily could have charged me with underage drinking and my friend's parents most definitely could have pressed charges against me and my family for what happened to their daughter, but none were filed. Now that I can examine the events of that night with some perspective, these are some of the insights I have gleaned. It is easy to see these events as a pure occurrence of coincidence, but I viewed them as orchestrated by God to send me a wake-up call to get my act together. I had to experience this in order to receive that dreaded warning when I could have avoided all of this if I had been wise enough to see the signs earlier. Why wait until you reach a breaking point or find yourself in a dangerous situation before you change the way you live? Most of us refuse to change because we are too complacent with our lives. How did complacency play into the events of that night? I did not believe that something like this could ever happen to me or my family; it was something I saw only in movies. My life was too comfortable and I depended on my parents' shield of protection as insurance from events like this.

Complacency can be so detrimental especially if one is not aware that they are in that state. I blocked out my friends and family from telling me things I did not want to hear so that I could continue living my life the way I wanted to. That March night was the culmination of my desire to do what I wanted with no regard to the possible consequences, yet through all of those events I realized that the God that I worship was relentless and ever merciful in his desire to transform my heart. A general misconception regarding Christianity is that the bible is a blueprint for righteous living, but nothing could be further from the truth. The bible is full of stories of unrighteous individuals that God pursues for his kingdom and how he intends to transform those individuals for righteous work in his kingdom. I fit right into the type of people that God pursued to change. No matter how many times I chose to follow my heart and do what I thought was good for myself, God was always right next to me through my pain, sorrow, happiness, and despair. Through every shameful act I participated in with my friends, God had been protecting me as his child, and no matter how many times I strayed away from him, he always chased me down relentlessly. Even when I had failed a thousand times, his mercy had endured and rescued me over and over again.

My intent is not to preach the gospel and compartmentalize all of my hardships into a call for you to receive the gospel, but my difficult journey would be incomplete if I excluded my faith in all of my endeavors. Even if you are not religious, you may have faced similar tribulations as I did with friendship. You may have disconnected with certain people to be friends with someone else or you may know someone who left you for another person. There is nothing wrong with wanting to branch out and make new friends. The harsh reality is that sometimes we need to change friends, not because our friends did anything wrong, but because life changes. Some friendships are not meant to last forever—this is inevitable. It is okay to mourn the loss of a friendship and move on to new friends. However, this change that causes us to move on must be a positive change. For me, the change was negative and was something that completely changed the course of my life for the worse. I tried so hard to be accepted by my trio of friends and I ended up doing things I was ashamed of.

In the immediate aftermath of that party, I was overcome with guilt to the point that I would not even go to church because I felt like a hypocrite and felt like I did not deserve to be my father's daughter. I tried to be someone I wasn't, and this tore me up from the inside out. Please don't ever feel like you have to change yourself to be accepted by a particular group. If this change is not driven by a desire for personal growth and improvement, you should rethink your priorities and make sure that you are being true to yourself. Why should you be the one to make changes to appease others at the expense of your own well-being and ideals? It is crucial to understand that your own peace is so much more valuable than constantly trying to please others, and that protecting your inner peace does not make you a selfish or arrogant person—it just means that you have respect and love for yourself and this is nothing you should be ashamed of.

PAST & PRESENT

Thanksgiving 2022 was when I was able to step foot in the beautiful island nation called Cuba. Initially, we had planned on going just as a family. However, one of our closest family friends expressed interest in exploring this beautiful island, so we all went together. All ten of us began preparing for our trip months in advance because this trip was going to be unlike any other. Because the United States has had no diplomatic relations with Cuba since the embargo of 1961, American citizens are unable to go on vacation to Cuba. A special visa must be obtained to enter the country and the trip must be more of a mission than a vacation. Many people have asked me why and how I was able to visit Cuba. Why would I want to go to a communist country that the United States has no official diplomatic relations with and where the travel restrictions are strict and irregular?

Going to Cuba was entirely my father's idea. According to him, movies such as *The Godfather Part II* painted a romantic picture of Cuba. His interest in visiting Cuba was piqued even further through all of the documentaries he would watch on Netflix regarding Cuba. As I watched from afar, I could see that he was consuming any and all documentaries about Cuba, including its cuisine and its history. His excitement was palpable, and I could tell that he was looking forward to this trip. While my brother and I always enjoyed traveling anywhere, my parents were far more interested in this trip than my brother and I were. We had no knowledge of Cuba and we had no intent of learning anything. We had just finished four months of school and the last thing we wanted to do was watch or read any sort of educational material about Cuba. We winged it and let our father explain away and we retained what we wanted.

We stayed one night in Miami before we flew out to Cuba. The humidity in Miami was intense, but it paled in comparison to what we were going to experience in Cuba. The minute we stepped off the airplane, we were hit hard with a jolt of humidity and heat. All of us were wearing long sleeves and long pants because it was cold in Arizona and on the airplane, but as soon as we stepped onto Cuban soil, we wanted to change into tank tops and shorts. Most of the world deals with humidity to some degree, but I emphasize the humidity because we do not have any in Arizona, which is why we all had such difficulty dealing with it during our stay in Cuba. Once we accepted that the weather was vastly different than in Arizona, it was time to explore this country.

In the days leading up to our trip, my father repeatedly emphasized two things as he was trying to teach us about Cuba. He spoke about Cuba being one of the world's few remaining communist countries and how the United States' 1962 embargo against Cuba is a crucial part of Cuba's identity. As we began exploring Cuba from the moment we entered its airspace, I began to see how these two factors were intertwined with the daily lives of all Cubans.

Jose Marti International Airport in Havana, Cuba's largest airport, was one of the most interesting airports I have ever been to. Having been to over twenty-two countries, I have seen my share of airports, but this one was unique. The buildings and walls were comically colorful and the color schemes did not match at all. The overall vibe was not that of an airport in 2022, but I felt like I was on a movie set from the 1940s. After about thirty minutes of navigating customs and reuniting with our luggage, we were greeted by our tour guide near the parking lot. In addition to the many airports I have been to, I have also dealt with many tour guides, and our Cuban guide was one of the best I have been around. He went out of his way to make our trip as enjoyable as it was, and I am grateful for that.

The ten of us boarded a huge yellow van and we headed to our first destination: the Plaza de Armas. This plaza was an opportunity for us to simply be in awe of the beautiful and magnificent buildings of central Havana. As we drove around the city, it didn't take long for me to notice the bright and classic American cars roaming the streets. These cars were unlike any other cars I had ever seen and truly were mesmerizing. In America, we rarely see cars from the 1950s on the streets with regularity, yet in Cuba, these cars were on every street corner. The infrastructure was also unique and haunting. The architecture was beautiful, but it seemed like every building was on the verge of collapsing at any moment. It felt as if the city had stopped developing after 1960 and I was transported to that time period through a time machine. I have been to many countries that would be considered underdeveloped, so I have seen my share of buildings on the verge of collapse. The scenery of the streets alone gave me optimism about the upcoming week we would be spending on this beautiful island.

After checking into our home base in Havana, we drove west to Pinar del Rio, the region of Cuba where 90 percent of its cigars are grown and produced. A handsome young man took us to an open shack and proceeded to deliver his presentation about the process of producing a cigar, from the many different types of tobacco leaves that went into a single cigar to how we must light the cigar to experience the quality of the cigar to the fullest. I enjoyed my time in this village, but smoking cigars was not for me because the smell was not pleasant.

That night, we drove back to Havana and were getting ready for a night at the Buena Vista Social Club, where we would be having dinner and drinks and seeing a musical ensemble show that would resemble a cabaret. The food was amazing and the performances were awesome. The culture of Cuba was on full display in the form of salsa music, a genre that can trace its origins to Cuba. All of the excitement from that night came to an end for me when I began drinking a nonalcoholic piña colada with tap water ice cubes, something we were advised not to consume. As soon as we got back to our residence, I headed straight to the restroom to appease my upset stomach. That first night, the pain was unbearable as if there were worms and parasites eating away at the lining of my stomach. My stomach never fully recovered throughout the remainder of our stay in Cuba, so I was not able to enjoy it as much as I could have. However, many amazing memories were waiting for me as we continued to explore this fascinating country.

Although my digestive issues hampered my stay in Cuba, I was still able to enjoy the scenery and the interactions I had with the people we met. One of the most interesting people we met was a University of Havana political science professor. Three months prior to our trip to Cuba, I had founded the first Model United Nations (MUN) chapter at my high school. I did this not only because the debates and discourses within MUN were robust and interesting, but because the values that the United Nations (UN) upholds are near and dear to me. These values are manifest in many UN policy decisions involving global security, nuclear proliferation, drug trafficking, and climate change. The spirit of MUN is to learn how countries can become allies to formulate conflict resolution strategies, and Cuba, with its rich and rugged political history, seemed like the prime example of a place that needed conflict resolution. The professor was the ideal person to have dinner with, and that is exactly what was arranged through our tour guide.

He is an expert in Cuban politics and has served in many capacities internationally on behalf of Cuba. He had also served Cuba in the UN before becoming a professor at the University of Havana. I peppered him with questions about Cuba's history and its people, and as our dinnertime conversations delved deeper into the issues that affected Cuba, my interest in international

relations in general grew. He talked extensively about the Embargo Act of 1962 instituted by President John F. Kennedy, a proclamation by the United States to restrict the exportation and importation of goods to and from Cuba. The manifestations of this embargo have reached every aspect of Cuban life, according to the professor. This was fascinating to me because I never could have imagined that events that transpired sixty years ago could have such a lasting impact in the future. I found myself appreciating history as a whole more after our dinner conversation with the professor.

When we turned in for the night, I began thinking about some of the major historical events I had learned about—World War II, the terrorist attacks of 9/11, the Civil Rights Act of 1964, and the Emancipation Proclamation. I never was a student of history because I never felt the effects of these historic events in my daily life—I went to school, I had dinner, I hung out with friends, and I lived my life comfortably. I also learned about how public perception of historic figures can have a wide spectrum. Fidel Castro bore the brunt of the blame for the embargo, yet he is also hailed as the hero of Cuba who stood up to American imperialism. Many younger Cubans and Cuban Americans blame Castro for the lack of infrastructure in Cuba, but many older Cubans, including the professor, praise Castro as the man who ousted the brutal regime of dictator Fulgencio Bautista, taking power out of the hands of foreign imperialists and putting it back into the hands of the Cuban people.

How we view Cuba will never be black and white, and the issues that plague Cubans, whether imagined or real, will not be resolved overnight. But as we dove into Cuban culture, the haunting romanticism of a country seemingly left behind in the 1950s opened my eyes to the importance of history. The past will always influence the present and dictate the future. Why is this so important? Every decision we make will influence what happens for generations to come. The choices I make today will not only affect my future, but the future of my grandchildren. I need to live with a sense of purpose that my decisions and actions can have a profound impact on society. I am forever grateful that I was able to figure this out in Cuba.

BE READY SO YOU DON'T HAVE TO GET READY

Traveling to Tanzania was a different type of mission than exploring Cuba. We found ourselves in this beautiful East African country through our church's short-term mission trip. My parents were the youth pastors of our church and they made an effort to organize a short-term mission trip every year. We were not able to go anywhere in 2020 and 2021 due to the pandemic, but for the summer of 2022, we were able to organize a mission trip to Tanzania. We had ten students on our team, including my brother and me, and we spent two weeks ministering to students, participating in Vacation Bible School, and fellowshipping with the students who were working with our host missionary in Morogoro, Tanzania.

Preparing for this trip was not easy at all. Our church held numerous fundraisers and we students put in countless hours into perfecting our skits and dance routines. Every Sunday after church, for four straight months, we had prayer meetings, language training, and study sessions of Tanzanian culture. We practiced singing and dancing for our body worship. My parents worked with other parents to pack large boxes full of donation items and equipment that we would need for our ministry efforts. We did not want to leave any stones unturned and wanted this trip to go as smoothly as possible. We felt that we were well prepared, but from the moment we arrived at the airport, things got off to a rocky start.

The ten of us arrived early at the airport with twenty-seven pieces of luggage. Our flight out of Phoenix was initially to Salt Lake City, and from there we were going to take a nine-hour flight to Amsterdam. From Amsterdam, we would catch the final flight to Dar es Salaam, Tanzania, our final destination. When we got to the ticket counter in Phoenix, we were told that our flight out of Salt Lake City was canceled and given our travel options. The attendant actually suggested that we cancel the trip and rebook the tickets for one week later! My mother and father looked at the attendant incredulously and asked how we could do that when we had our schedule all planned out in Tanzania, not to mention handling twenty-seven pieces of luggage and adjusting the schedule of fourteen people with fourteen different plans for the summer. The mission almost ended before it began. There was one flight From Salt Lake City to Amsterdam, but that plane would have already departed thirty minutes before we landed in Salt Lake City. As Christians who believe that God would somehow make a way when there seemed to be none, we decided in faith to fly to Salt Lake City and see what options were available.

When we arrived in Salt Lake City, we were informed of another flight that was en route to Amsterdam, but once again we would miss the direct flight to Dar es Salaam from Amsterdam and that there was no guarantee that we could find a connecting flight to our destination. Again we decided to put our faith in God and boarded this flight to Amsterdam, hoping that while we were in the air a path would form to get to Tanzania. Through the grace of God, we were able to board a plane that would fly from Amsterdam to Dubai, and from Dubai out to Dar es Salaam. Through all of the uncertainty, we were finally going to Tanzania twenty-four hours later than our original ETA. All we could rely on was our prayers because we could do nothing to improve our chances of getting to our destination; we were at the mercy of the airlines and their constantly changing schedule. We had just endured our first of many trials and the trip hadn't even started yet.

When we finally arrived in Tanzania, we were faced with yet another issue. Only some of our luggage had arrived. There were fourteen of us and we left Phoenix with twenty-seven pieces of luggage, yet only seventeen pieces of our luggage arrived in Tanzania. We had no idea where the other ten pieces ended up—Amsterdam, Dubai, or Zanzibar during our brief stopover there. Before we even left the airport in Dar es Salaam, all of the clothing and accessories I had packed were gone and we had no idea where it was. I remember the enraged look on my brother's face as we discovered that all of his clothes were missing. We were all tired, frustrated, and hungry and didn't know what to do. We stood in front of the baggage claim, patiently waiting for any good news as the adults were talking with the front desk. The missionary we were working with in Tanzania waited patiently for us to figure this mess out. After two hours of waiting at the airport with no answers, my parents came up to the group and said that we would have to continue on with this trip without our luggage. We were on this trip on a mission for God. How could God let this happen to us? What did we do to deserve this? What was really frustrating was that the four members of our group who lost all of their personal luggage were me, my brother, my mother, and my father! I was on a mission to share the gospel and I could feel nothing but anger and frustration before we even began our ministry. However, it was all going to be for a greater purpose and I was soon going to learn what it meant to have faith in a God who could move mountains for the greater good of evangelism.

After we accepted that the luggage was lost and we were going to continue on, we boarded our bus with our host missionary and drove to the largest shopping mall to grab a bite to eat and shop to replace some of the items we had lost. We had to purchase underwear, socks, toiletries, and other basic necessaries. My father had the experience of shopping for hair gel in a place where he was the minority shopping for a product that was not readily available. In America, the variety of hair products in any store was for the convenience of anyone not African American. In Africa, the hair products for nonblack individuals were not readily available and, for the first time ever, my father got a glimpse of what it was like to be a minority, even if it involved something as insignificant as trying to obtain hair gel. After we finished shopping and had a sumptuous lunch of fried chicken, we embarked on the four-hour drive from Dar es Salaam to Morogoro.

When we arrived in Morogoro, we were invited to the host missionary's house, where we would review our schedule for the next week. What greeted us at their house was a beautiful sight for sore eyes—a warm and comforting Korean dinner waiting for us in the living room. The missionary's wife had prepared an extravagant meal for all of us as a treat for making it this far, and we were all so relieved to see kimchi after not eating it for only two days. After having fellowship over a wonderful meal, we headed to our lodging at the Presbyterian seminary. The rooms were dormitories for the seminary students and because it was the summer, most of the rooms were empty. Inside every room was a piece of furniture that was never more welcome for me—a large, white mosquito net covering each bed. I hate mosquitoes with a passion and I was so grateful that these nets would protect me from those bloodsuckers for the time I stayed there. Because there was no warm water and the water pressure was nonexistent, I took a cold shower under dripping water and I loved every minute of it after going two whole days without washing at all. I actually developed an affinity for cold showers after this experience in Tanzania, and I went to sleep that night still holding out hope that our luggage would be found and delivered to our dorm the next day.

The next day, we began our multifaceted ministry in six different villages scattered through the greater Morogoro area. We engaged in fellowship with the students from the seminary and youths from the churches we visited, all of whom were planted by our host missionary. We were able to experience many of the cultures within Tanzania, particularly that of the Maasai tribe. We were guests of honor at the Maasai church and were treated to a ceremony on our behalf, and we enjoyed another hearty meal that consisted of a whole cow butchered specifically for that occasion. If everything I had planned had gone wrong for this trip, the one thing that went exactly according to plan was our ministry. We nailed our skit and our dance moves, and we were so blessed with all of the new friends we made. I then realized that this was God's plan all along. He wanted to eliminate all of the extracurricular activities that I had looked forward to, the pictures on the pristine beaches with my new dress, and he wanted me to focus on what the purpose of my trip was. It worked. As we began to wind down our ministry and looked forward to relaxing for a few days, I felt blessed that everything had happened as it had.

One of the first leisurely activities we were able to participate in was to go on a safari. On the third day of our stay, our group got a taste of what a safari was like. We got up early in the morning and got into these large safari vehicles as we headed to Mikumi National Park. Our end goal was to see the Big Five animals in Africa: the lion, elephant, leopard, African buffalo, and rhinoceros. Although we didn't get to see all five, we did get to see the king of the jungle, the lion, which is what we ultimately came for. Seeing how free the animals were in their natural habitat almost brought tears to my eyes. Zoos and aquariums may be rehabilitating injured animals and they genuinely are trying to protect these animals. However, many of those animals are held against their will, and they were never meant to live in captivity. Lions were not designed to be kept in cages behind bars for our entertainment, and seeing how the lion and lioness roamed around freely made me tremble. There is a reason lions are called the king of the jungle, and that reason became very apparent in the way they walked, breathed, and roared.

Watching these animals in their natural habitat the way they were supposed to be seen made me realize how manipulative humans can be with animals for their own pleasure. The zebras' stripes in Africa looked much healthier and more fully coated than what we would see in a zoo. This safari was proof that animals thrive overall when they are not being held captive, and I felt so blessed to be able to see these animals the way they were meant to be seen. This was Tanzania for me: a spiritual battle of ups and downs and an experience that raised in me a greater awareness of wildlife conservation. In the midst of my revelations about wildlife, the luggage I had been praying would be delivered to us in Tanzania was ultimately located and returned not to us in the mission field, but to our home in Arizona.

What made Tanzania so special was what we as a group endured in order to make this trip the best it could be, and I believe that God used this trip to show me how little faith I had in him. All my life, I had been told to pray and have faith in God, that he would listen to my prayers. However, when I was actually dealt a situation where all I could do was pray, I struggled hard to do so. There is something for everyone to learn from this experience whether you are religious or not, and that is that no matter how much you prepare for something in life, you will never be completely ready for it. Whatever it is you are pursuing in life right now, don't get ready for it; be ready for it. I was so sure that I was 100 percent prepared for everything and anything that came at me during this mission trip, yet the unthinkable happened. My luggage got lost, there were mosquitoes that even repellents couldn't get rid of, and my flight got canceled. Could I have controlled any of these things? The answer is a resounding no. However, these situations tested my ability to adapt. I believe that the ability to adapt to changing environments and situations is one of the best skills to have, because that is what life will throw at you. You should live your life expecting things to go completely south, and you may find yourself embracing new opportunities in life that you never would have been exposed to if everything went according to plan.

I CHOOSE COMPASSION

Nika is a Ukrainian high school student I met when I went to Senftenberg, Germany. My family and I had the opportunity of meeting her and other students at a refugee camp for Ukrainians who were forced to evacuate their homes due to Russia's invasion of Ukraine. We worked with a missionary serving in Germany, to provide the students with a three-day Vacation Bible School where we played fun games, made arts and crafts, and danced to worship music together. Those three days of fellowship were full of pure joy, youth, and innocence, and getting to know the students on a personal level taught me many things about myself and about friendship. Although I enjoyed connecting with all of the students there, Nika was the one I bonded with the most because she was one of the few students who was the same age as me.

Although we became friends, it wasn't until the last day that she opened up to me about the conflicts that she had been facing since moving to Germany. Nika expressed to me that there were many Muslims at school who would bully her and pick on her for being a refugee. They would ask her things like, "Is Putin your favorite person on earth?" Nika told me that she would ignore these foolish jokes and comments and think to herself, "Why do they think it's appropriate to ask me these questions? I had to leave my home and my grandparents behind; of course he is not my favorite person!"

Nika told me that she missed her bedroom in Ukraine because in Germany, she had to share a room with her sister and the rooms were very small. Nika had also mentioned that she attended German school in the morning and Ukrainian school with the other refugees in the evening so that when it was time to go back to their country, they would not be behind on their education. Hearing all of this from her was eye-opening because everything I had heard on the news about Ukraine and Russia became personal. I had always heard stories about the impacts of war on people; however, this was the first time I had ever seen this influence in person. Watching the news in my living room about Ukrainian refugees and hearing Nika talk to me about her own personal stories from this war was a sobering experience. All I could do was listen and empathize with her.

Because this was the last day I would be seeing Nika and the rest of the students, I gave her a hug and added her on all social media platforms. Early the next morning, I received a direct message from Nika. She asked me if she could stop by the hotel I was staying at and give me something. On her way to school in the morning, she walked from her house to my hotel and handed me a gift bag. She wanted to thank me and my family for coming to Germany to spend time with her and the rest of the Ukrainian community. I was overcome with gratitude not only for the gift, but also for the opportunity God gave me to make a new friend. The heartfelt letter that Nika had written moved me to tears. To me, what my family and I had to offer seemed insignificant to the students. We were unsure if they were going to like half of the things we prepared for them, but everything ended up working out. To hear about how much Nika enjoyed this camp made me feel relieved that God was working the entire time. This new bond that I created with Nika reminded me of the true meaning of friendship. To be able to care for someone and know more about them and identify with them is what makes a strong friendship. As I saw things from a different perspective while talking to Nika, I was reminded how important it is to lead with a compassionate and empathetic heart. People desire to feel heard and understood, and this experience proved to me that true friendship occurs when both sides of the party can do so as a means to promote feelings of connection. Nika and I continue to keep in touch today through Snapchat and Instagram, and I continue to pray for her and her family so that they may reunite with their loved ones back at home in Ukraine.

A DIVE INTO THE ABYSS

Our family took a trip to Cancun in 2016 when I was ten years old. If I were to describe this vacation in three words, they would be *blessed*, *informative*, and *adventurous*. Cancun was the first place I experienced and tasted an exotic and foreign culture for the first time, which is why I think the memories I have are still so vivid in my mind today. From trying a piña colada (nonalcoholic) to swimming with whale sharks out in the ocean, this trip is still the most memorable and enjoyable of all the trips I have been on. Everything about the city was as beautiful as advertised, especially the beautiful waters that surrounded the island. But more so than the beautiful landscape, it was an encounter with a few beautiful ocean creatures that really put things in perspective. We had similar encounters with some other creatures when we visited the big island of Hawaii in 2018, and both experiences taught me a valuable lesson about life.

My brother and I woke up to the sound of the booming alarm at 5:30 a.m. I put my swimsuit on and attempted to go back to sleep, but was woken up by my mother smothering sunscreen all over my body. When we were all dressed and ready to go, we got into the taxi for a thirty-minute ride down to the shore. I was comfortable in my swimsuit, but when we arrived at the dock, they told us that we would have to wear wetsuits. With the help of my mother, I stretched the tight wetsuit to fit my body. I felt claustrophobic inside of it. It was a hot summer day, and the feeling of a thick, leather-like swimsuit covering my entire body was unsettling. By the time we were on the boat, I was still incredibly tired. My eyes were so close to being shut and my brain could not process the fact that we were on a boat in Cancun at seven in the morning. It was a two-hour boat ride to get to our snorkeling destination, so I took that opportunity to take a nap.

I woke up an hour later, and as soon as I opened my eyes and my brain started functioning again, I felt like throwing up. The crashing waves and wicked winds made it a bumpy boat ride and I immediately got seasick. Not only was I sweating profusely in my wetsuit that felt like it was made for a toddler, but I also felt like I could vomit at any time. My mother kept telling me to look far off into the distance, but being the obstinate child I was, I ignored her and sat there with an angry expression on my face. I was grumpy and wanted to go home. When the boat finally came to a stop, everyone on the boat, including the rest of my family, was dressed from head to toe in their snorkeling gear except for me. I felt too ill to jump into the water, so I decided to stay on the boat with the driver. He offered me peanuts and pretzels. I snacked on those while the boat driver gave me tips on how to get rid of my motion sickness. The driver told me that I would feel ten times better if I jumped into the water because then I would be moving with the water and wouldn't be sitting still like I would be if I were on the boat. To be frank, I thought the driver was a very attractive man and I had developed a crush on him when he first held my hand to help me get on the boat at the very start of the trip. So I listened and put on my flippers, life vest, goggles, and mouthpiece and jumped into the water with no hesitation. I swam toward my parents. They were shocked to see me in the water with them.

"Look under the water, Katherine!" my father shouted at me.

I sprang into the blue abyss and felt complete serenity when I did. I dipped my head under the water and there it was. My head went down and then there was silence. I was staring into the incredible deep blue water while floating on the surface with my head submerged. A dark form suddenly came nearer, greater in size than anything I could have imagined. Nothing could have prepared me for the first whale shark I would encounter, which was swiftly followed by roughly nine more of his traveling companions. I felt as though I was floating among various gray and dark planets for a brief period of time while I was suspended in my own galaxy. That sense of indifference and frailty was initially alarming. Before I knew it, I was eye to eye with the gentle giant. We locked eyes and looked into one another. Those enormous and intelligent eyes reflected my curiosity, intrigue, and wonder. I was staring in awe at a creature that is so mysterious yet so recognizable. I wanted to preserve this memory yet feel what I felt all over again because of how overwhelming it was. I carried this unforgettable encounter with a beautiful creature over into another similar yet unique experience I had in Hawaii just short two years later.

You would think that I would have learned to look beyond the horizon to avoid getting seasick on boats, but I made the exact same mistake in Hawaii when we rode off into the ocean to see some sea creatures reminiscent of what we had seen in Cancun. This time, our voyage to the ocean was at night, which made me feel even worse. Motion sickness has truly been the enemy of all of my vacations, but I wasn't going to let it ruin my stay in Hawaii. When the boat came to a stop, I was actually the first to dive into the water even though I felt incredibly ill because I could not contain my excitement. When I dove into the water, I found my way to the large raft that had handles for us to hold on to while we viewed the sea creatures swim beneath us. The creatures we were going to see were manta rays. A large light was attached to the bottom of the raft to shine light on the plankton in the ocean so that the animals would be attracted to it. My family and I held onto the raft's handles patiently waiting for some life-form to pass us by, but there was nothing. Those fifteen minutes of waiting in the ocean's cold waters did not help ease my motion sickness. By then, I really felt like I was going to throw up.

All of a sudden, another group of people on a different raft yelled out of excitement and told everyone to look below them. It was right at the moment when the sea creatures were beneath us that I threw up in the ocean, half of it going straight into my father's hair. Thankfully, he had his head submerged under water and didn't even notice that my vomit had gone into his hair. I had just thrown up uncontrollably yet I could not wait to see what everyone was looking at, so I immediately put on my goggles and saw two gigantic manta rays swimming around me. I was overcome with astonishment and surprise because these immense creatures came much closer and their acrobatics were much more breathtaking than anticipated.

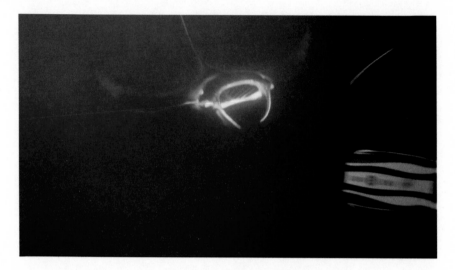

When we think about angels, we typically visualize their gorgeous wings and the peace, vitality, and sense of completion they give us. I am convinced that manta rays are the angels of the sea, as they give us a spiritual experience akin to meeting an angel and they leave us feeling fully at one with nature. Swimming with these manta rays was a humbling and emotional roller coaster with a very beautiful and uplifting conclusion. People crave a chance to enjoy nature at its finest, and these gentle giants provided that experience for me and for many others who have enjoyed their company in the waters.

These are the moments in life that leave you speechless and are difficult to describe with words. You feel overpowered and dazed since they are unlike anything else you have encountered in your life. These moments are more substantial than what words or images can convey and are so much more than just a physical encounter. These indescribable experiences are the ones that alter your life completely. The magical moments with the whale sharks and with the manta rays motivated me to conserve the environment and continue exploring the ocean. Staring into the whale shark's eyes made me feel compelled to do whatever it takes to make a difference in bettering these creatures' homes. These experiences taught me that connections with nature and the ocean are the finest conceivable reasons for wanting to protect the environment. You may not be swimming with manta rays or whale sharks anytime soon. However, I hope that you do those magical things that you cannot fully describe with an Instagram post or a conversation. Whatever it may entail for you, go out there and do something that is beyond words in its personalness. In the end, these encounters will spur you on to keep looking for those untamed, enchanted, and salty regions of every corner of the world. And when you are encouraged to do so, my prayer is that you will continue to fight to keep them safe for future generations.

AFTERWORD

As I shared my stories with underserved students in Phoenix at the nonprofit organizations I volunteered at, the students became drawn to what I had to say. They were inspired that their trials and tribulations did not have to serve as obstacles to their success in life or their desire to serve the community, and they became motivated to overcome those hurdles in their lives. What seemed insignificant and unimportant to me was interesting to the students I was working with, and this allowed me to realize that what I had experienced was not ordinary. While I thought I was helping them with their needs, little did I know that they would play a role in helping me step out of my comfort zone to express myself and stepping into a new adventure of writing a book. I learned how one person can change the atmosphere of a community and bring positive light to the people of that community. I saw how a little hope and encouragement can have an impact on someone's life and change their attitude. I also experienced the joy of sharing the contents of my heart and building relationships. I learned that those things I believed to be small gravel, my anecdotes and struggles, can collectively be used to not only build a wall, but an entire shelter that can give rise to more empowered people. I want to continue to grow academically, mentally, and spiritually to bring light and hope into someone's darkness. I would love to continue to travel, write, and create more memories and life experiences that I could share with new people.

ACKNOWLEDGMENT

I give all thanks and praise to God, who has been there with me at every step of my journey of life. God called me as his child and adopted me into his kingdom family. He designed me and knew me even before I was born. God has provided me with the resources to achieve this accomplishment and has allowed me the wisdom and knowledge to produce this book. I am truly grateful for his unconditional love and mercy, and for the grace he has extended to me and my family.

To my beloved parents, Thomas and Rina, thank you for all of your sacrifice and support. You two have shaped me into who I am. I am so grateful for both of you and for all the memories we've created and shared. Thank you for your guidance, protection, direction, comfort, and wisdom. You two truly accept me and love me for who I am, and I am so appreciative of your patience. I want to thank my father especially for being the backbone of all that I do. You have directed so much of your time and effort to helping me with whatever I needed and you have never hesitated to drop what you were doing and put my needs above yours. I thank God for giving me two extraordinary parents.